W9-BWL-572

Eating Well

Crabtree Publishing Company

www.crabtreebooks.com

Crabtree Publishing Company

www.crabtreebooks.com   1-800-387-7650

Published in Canada
Crabtree Publishing
616 Welland Ave.
St. Catharines, ON
L2M 5V6

Published in the United States
Crabtree Publishing
PMB16A
350 Fifth Ave., Suite 3308
New York, NY 10118

Senior editor
Jennifer Schofield

Proofreader
Crystal Sikkens

Designer
Sophie Pelham

Project coordinator
Robert Walker

Digital color
Carl Gordon

Production coordinator
Margaret Amy Salter

Editor
Molly Aloian

Prepress technician
Katherine Kantor

Copy editor
Adrianna Morganelli

First published in 2008 by Wayland
338 Euston Road
London NW1 3BH

Wayland Australia
Level 17/207 Kent Street
Sydney NSW 2000

Copyright © Wayland 2008

Wayland is a division of
Hachette Children's Books,
a Hachette Livre UK company.

Library and Archives Canada Cataloguing in Publication

Gogerly, Liz
      Eating well / Liz Gogerly ; illustrator, Mike Gordon.

(Looking after me)
Includes index.
ISBN 978-0-7787-4110-7 (bound).--ISBN 978-0-7787-4117-6 (pbk.)

      1. Nutrition--Juvenile fiction. 2. Health--Juvenile fiction.
I. Gordon, Mike II. Title. III. Series: Gogerly, Liz. Looking after me.

PZ7.G562Ea 2008   j823'.92   C2008-903648-4

Library of Congress Cataloging-in-Publication Data

Gogerly, Liz.
      Eating well / written by Liz Gogerly ; illustrated by Mike Gordon.
            p. cm. -- (Looking after me)
      Includes index.
      ISBN-13: 978-0-7787-4117-6 (pbk. : alk. paper)
      ISBN-10: 0-7787-4117-6 (pbk. : alk. paper)
      ISBN-13: 978-0-7787-4110-7 (reinforced library binding : alk. paper)
      ISBN-10: 0-7787-4110-9 (reinforced library binding : alk. paper)
      1. Nutrition--Juvenile literature. I. Gordon, Mike, ill. II. Title. III. Series.

      RA784.G575 2009
      613.2--dc22
                                                                        2008025342

Looking After Me

Eating Well

Written by Liz Gogerly
Illustrated by Mike Gordon

I loved staying at my friend
Ethan's house.

We ate the best snacks ever!

At lunchtime, Ethan's family ate the greatest food in the world.

But, best of all, we were allowed to eat in front of the television.

Later, we always had a midnight snack.
But, it wasn't always fun and games.

The last time
I went to Ethan's
house, we ate
so much that
I was sick.

My stomach felt
like it was going
to explode.

I dreamed about the future, too...

When I grow up, I don't want to be unhealthy.

I want to be strong —
just like my dad.

I want to feel good...

...and have
a lot of
energy.

12

Dad said that one of the secrets of staying fit and healthy is eating well.

I went to school with
a spring in my step.

At lunchtime, I ate my sandwich and yogurt and drank some ice-cold water.

That afternoon, I whizzed through my work. My teacher was really pleased with me.

But, best of all,

I scored two
goals in our
soccer match!

I felt great and I wanted Ethan
to feel good about himself, too.
The secret is to eat well.

Everyone needs plenty of fresh fruit and vegetables – five a day.

Chuck the chips!

Instead, try
brown bread,

pasta,
rice, and
potatoes.

20

Eat fresh fish, lean meat, chicken, beans, nuts, and seeds.

Cheese, yogurt, and milk are good for your bones and teeth.

Eat a balanced diet,

and you'll
be fit, healthy,
and strong.

Soon, Ethan changed his ways.
Now he eats healthy food nearly
all the time.

But sometimes he likes a
special treat and so do I!

Now Ethan feels great!
He's taught me something
about food, too...

that it's fun
to grow your
own vegetables.

These days I love
good food.

I can even grow
some of my own.

I like to try new
things all the time...
Well, not always,
but I'm getting
better every day.

NOTES FOR PARENTS AND TEACHERS

SUGGESTIONS FOR READING
LOOKING AFTER ME: EATING WELL
WITH CHILDREN

Eating Well is the story of two typical young boys, James and Ethan, with a healthy appetite for unhealthy food. It begins with a sleepover at Ethan's house. James is delighted that Ethan's family eats food such as chips, hamburgers, and pizzas. He's also excited that they eat while they watch television – something he's possibly not allowed to do in his own home. This is a good place to stop and ask the children what they think of the kind of food that Ethan's family eats. Do they think it is healthy or unhealthy? Why is it so? What do they think about eating and watching the television at the same time? It is also a good place to discuss the importance of eating as a family. Do they ever eat at a table with the rest of their family?

The story goes on to show the consequences of the boys' unhealthy midnight snack. Again, this is a chance to discuss how eating unhealthy foods might affect people's general well-being. James is lucky he just feels sick because there are many worse illnesses that can be caused by eating unhealthy food. The children may have examples from their own lives that they can add to the discussion.

Fortunately, as the story progresses, James and Ethan learn about eating healthy and they discover the many benefits of a balanced diet. The story has plenty of opportunities to stop and talk about the children's own diets. What foods do they like? Do they think they eat a healthy diet?

Do they know about the different food groups and what makes up a good, balanced diet? What kinds of food help people to grow strong bones and teeth? The story also touches on eating the occasional treat. It is important that children realize that some foods are not very healthy but that it is alright to eat them in moderation.

LOOKING AFTER ME AND CURRICULUM EXPECTATIONS

The Looking After Me series is designed to teach young readers the importance of personal hygiene, proper nutrition, exercise, and personal safety. This series supports key K-4 health education standards in Canada and the United States, including those outlined by the American Association for Health Education. According to these standards, students will

- Describe relationships between personal health behaviors and individual well being
- Explain how childhood injuries and illnesses can be prevented or treated
- Identify responsible health behaviors
- Identify personal health needs
- Demonstrate strategies to improve or maintain personal health
- Demonstrate ways to avoid and reduce threatening situations

BOOKS TO READ

The Monster Health Book Edward Miller (Holiday House, 2006)
Oliver's Fruit Salad Vivian French (Hodder Children's Books, 1998)
Oliver's Vegetables Vivian French (Hodder Children's Books, 1995)

ACTIVITY

The Healthy Shopping Game

This is a game that tests both memory and the ability to think of healthy foods that begin with a certain letter of the alphabet. The first person to go has to select an item that begins with 'a'. He or she would say something like, 'I went to the store and bought myself an apple.' The next person to go would think of food that starts with 'b' and say something like, 'I went to the store and bought myself an apple and some beans'. The next person would select an item beginning with 'c' and so on.

INDEX

beans 21
bread 20
breakfast 13
burgers 5

cheese 21
chicken 21
chips 5, 20

fish 21
fruit 19, 24

junk food 8

lunch 5, 15

meat 21
milk 21

nuts 21

pasta 20
potatoes 20

rice 20

sandwiches 15
seeds 21
snacks 4, 6

vegetables 19, 27

water 15

yogurt 15, 21

Printed in China